Camel Spider

A Camel Spider Pet Owner's Guide

Camel Spider Facts and Descriptions, Choosing and Acquiring, Breeding, Feeding, Care Requirements, Molting, and Housing All Included!

By: Lolly Brown

Copyrights and Trademarks

All rights reserved. No part of this book may be reproduced or transformed in any form or by any means, graphic, electronic, or mechanical, including photocopying, recording, taping, or by any information storage retrieval system, without the written permission of the author.

This publication is Copyright ©2021 NRB Publishing, an imprint of Pack & Post Plus, LLC. Nevada. All products, graphics, publications, software and services mentioned and recommended in this publication are protected by trademarks. In such instance, all trademarks & copyright belong to the respective owners. For information consult www.NRBpublishing.com

Disclaimer and Legal Notice

This product is not legal, medical, or accounting advice and should not be interpreted in that manner. You need to do your own due-diligence to determine if the content of this product is right for you. While every attempt has been made to verify the information shared in this publication, neither the author, neither publisher, nor the affiliates assume any responsibility for errors, omissions or contrary interpretation of the subject matter herein. Any perceived slights to any specific person(s) or organization(s) are purely unintentional.

We have no control over the nature, content and availability of the web sites listed in this book. The inclusion of any web site links does not necessarily imply a recommendation or endorse the views expressed within them. We take no responsibility for, and will not be liable for, the websites being temporarily unavailable or being removed from the internet.

The accuracy and completeness of information provided herein and opinions stated herein are not guaranteed or warranted to produce any particular results, and the advice and strategies, contained herein may not be suitable for every individual. Neither the author nor the publisher shall be liable for any loss incurred as a consequence of the use and application, directly or indirectly, of any information presented in this work. This publication is designed to provide information in regard to the subject matter covered.

Neither the author nor the publisher assume any responsibility for any errors or omissions, nor do they represent or warrant that the ideas, information, actions, plans, suggestions contained in this book is in all cases accurate. It is the reader's responsibility to find advice before putting anything written in this book into practice. The information in this book is not intended to serve as legal, medical, or accounting advice.

Foreword

Before buying any pet, it is important to know that as a pet owner you are responsible for the care and wellbeing of your pet. It is important to try and learn as much as you can about the animal you are seeing to keep as a pet to make sure that your household, financial status and lifestyle are suited to provide your pet with the best possible care. This book has been designed to provide you with both concise and precise information about a Camel spider basic needs to help you provide your pet with the best quality care practices.

As with all pet ownership, new and improved products will come on the market and sometimes even the best practice guidelines for caring for your animal may change. It is important therefore to see this book as your gateway to a continuous learning program of Camel spider ownership and ensure that you are updating your knowledge and skills as a pet owner on a regular basis. You might be surprised at just how much is involved in caring for your tiny new family member, but I promise that it will be an enjoyable journey and you will find the answers to all your burning questions over the next few pages as I take you through every facet of being a responsible Camel spider owner.

Included inside this book's first section is about the descriptions and facts about a Camel spider. It also contains information about its appearance, behavior, habitat, life cycle, diet, predators and threats.

The Second section is about choosing and acquiring a Camel spider. It tackles things to consider before getting a Camel spider and how to select a healthy Camel spider pet.

The next section focuses on how you can cater your Camel spider's nutritional needs.

The fourth section will talk about the molting of your camel spider.

In the next section, you will learn how to provide an appropriate housing or enclosure for your Camel spider including all the essential tools that you must have.

The eighth section focuses on the common health issues of a Camel spider and how to deal with them.

For the last section, it will talk about the breeding process for your Camel spider and how to take care of the spiderlings.

You can start learning about this amazing animal on the pages that follow. And although you should never view a single source of information as a comprehensive guide, you should be better prepared to care for a Camel spider after finishing this book.

Table of Contents

Introduction 1

Chapter One: Camel Spider Facts and Descriptions 1

    Camel Spider Names 1

    Camel Spider Appearance and Behavior 2

    Camel Spider Habitat 4

    Lifecycle 4

    Camel Spider Diet 6

    Camel Spider Predators and Threats 7

Chapter Two: Choosing and Acquiring a Camel Spider 9

    Places to Find Camel Spider 9

        Shows and Expos 10

        Camel Spider Dealers 11

        The Internet 11

    Shipping and Transporting Camel Spiders 13

        Pet & Specialty Stores 13

    Choosing A Specific Camel Spider 14

Chapter Three: Feeding Your Camel Spider 17

    Learn about Your Spider's Meal Preferences 19

    Where to Acquire Meals 20

    Gut-loading Crickets and Roaches 20

Water 22

Chapter Four: Molting 23

Chapter Five: Housing for Your Camel Spider 27

    Setting Up Your Terrarium 27

        Escape Proofing 28

        Sun Tea Jars 28

        Critter Keepers 29

        Mason Jars 29

    Substrate 29

        Hiding Spots 30

    Decorations 30

    Heating 31

    Temperatures 31

        Thermometers 31

        Heat Pads 32

    Humidity 32

        For Terrariums with Mesh Lids 32

        Other Containers 33

    Lighting 34

    Sticks, Rocks, And Branches 34

        Sticks 35

        Branches 35

- Rocks 35
- Substrate And Groundcover 36
- Plants 37
- Housing Multiple Spiders 39
- Territory 39

Chapter Six: Vet Care for Your Camel Spider 41
- Health & First Aid 41
  - Bad Molts 41
  - Mites 43
  - Mold and Fungal Infections 44
  - Parasites 45
  - Wounds 46

Chapter Seven: Breeding Your Camel Spider 47
- Sexing 47
- Breeding 49
- Eggs and Spiderlings 54
- Egg Sacs 56
- Caring For Egg Sacs 61
- How Long Before Babies Become Visible? 62
- Housing 63
- Temperature 65
- Humidity 65

Food 66

Conclusion 67

Glossary of Terms 69

Index 91

Photo Credits 97

References 101

Introduction

Camel spiders can be amazing pets for many reasons. Unfortunately, they are not as popular as many other animals in the pet trade. Their unique behavior and body colors make them very attractive. They also don't require a lot of maintenance and can be purchased for an affordable price.

Most adult camel spiders can eat insects like crickets or fruit flies which are typically sold at most pet stores. Camel spiders are also known to be gentile around humans yet aggressive to their prey. They make as great first pet even for children. Children can learn a lot about the care and life cycle from them. Camel spiders also do not require attention from their owner and can be left alone for hours or even days. They don't need a large enclosure which makes them great for smaller homes or apartments.

Learn more about Camel Spiders in the next pages. Let's get started!

Chapter One: Camel Spider Facts and Descriptions

Camel Spider Names

From the Solpugidae family and the class Arachnida, the camel spider goes by other names such as sun spider, wind scorpion and Egyptian Giant solpugid. Sun Spider is from the Latin word "solpugid". But for this manuscript, we will use name "camel spider".

Chapter One: Camel Spider Facts and Descriptions

The name "camel spider" is from the myth that this creature eats the insides of a camel's stomach. But this is not actually true. The name just stuck with it despite the busted myth, making its name a bit misleading.

This creature has more than 1,000 species. *Galeodes caspius, Galeodes arab, Paragaleodes* and *Galeodes granti*, to name a few.

Camel Spider Appearance and Behavior

This creature is dark brown and tan in color with tiny hairs on its body. The fine and tiny hairs on its body is beneficial to insulate it from the heat of the desert. While its coloration helps it to blend into the hot and dry environment which makes it safe from its predators.

The camel spider has 8 legs. Some people were misguided thinking that it has ten because of its 2 elongated pedipalps (the appendages' second pair) which are located near its mouth. Camel spiders use these to search for its prey and pull in it.

Chapter One: Camel Spider Facts and Descriptions

A camel spider has typical size of 3-6 inches long. Its weight is about 2 ounces. By placing 3 golf tees on the ground end to end, you would picture the length of a six-inch camel spider. Meanwhile, if you hold a tennis ball in your hand, its about the same weight of a 2—ounce camel spider.

Camel spiders can move very fast through their scrubland or desert habitat. The fastest they can reach is about 10mph, which is only about one-fifth as quick as a rabbit.

There is a myth that camel spiders hunt human beings in order to bite them. The truth is that, the camel spider doesn't actually know it's following a person. It's just a person casts a long shadow. This creature enjoys the coolness of a person's shadow in the warm environment in which it lives.

Camel spiders are known to be solitary except during the mating period. These creatures can be hostile or aggressive is they feel threatened although they are infrequently seen by people since they are known the be nocturnal.

Chapter One: Camel Spider Facts and Descriptions

Camel Spider Habitat

Camel spiders are found in southwestern United States, Mexico and Middle East. They live in a hot and dry deserts and scrublands habitat.

These creatures hide in fissures between rocks and under logs to keep them cool when the temperature during the day reach its highest. They chase and hunt at night when the temperatures are cooler.

Because of the scarcity of eater in the desert, Camel spiders get most of its needed liquid to survive when they feed on their prey.

Camel spiders don't migrate. They live in a scrubland or desert in their entire short lives.

Lifecycle

The lifecycle of a camel spider lasts up to one year.

Eggs

Chapter One: Camel Spider Facts and Descriptions

All spiders begin as eggs. The mother constructs a special pod out of strong silk called an egg sac to keep her brood safe. A camel spider keeps her babies in her web to protect them. While she will not nurture it, she will stand guard by it. It can take anywhere from two weeks to a month and a half for the eggs to hatch. When this happens, the babies (called hatchlings) will break their way out.

Hatchlings

Hatchlings are born hairless, colorless, and cannot eat. They remain in the egg sac before actually emerging. After they have shed their first exoskeleton, they will come out.

Spiderlings

Camel spiderlings do not begin to eat until about a week after hatching, as their fangs are too weak and soft to eat. As soon as they are ready to feed, they will eat their weaker siblings. This cannibalism is completely normal – out of the five hundred babies born, only thirty are strong enough to survive. This sacrifice of the siblings allows other

Chapter One: Camel Spider Facts and Descriptions

generations to thrive. The mother will not care for her offspring, and she will ignore them.

Adult Spiders

Adult spiders can reproduce and create larger populations of camel spiders. Occasionally, they will molt and grow even larger. An adult female can produce ten egg sacs per mating, each sac containing 50-250 eggs.

Camel Spider Diet

Camel spiders are carnivores. Some of their prey includes termites, gerbils, beetles, lizards, snakes and small birds.

This creature can even eat a prey that is bigger than itself. Like many other animals, a camel spider will eat whatever prey is most abundant in its surroundings.

A camel spider uses its pedipalps to look and sense for a prey while it uses its jaw grab them. This arachnid uses its

Chapter One: Camel Spider Facts and Descriptions

own digestive juices to turn its prey to a liquid than it can consume.

Because there is not much food accessible for camel spiders in places in which they live, these creatures tend to store fats in their bodies to sustain them in time when they can find prey.

Camel Spider Predators and Threats

Some of the predators of a camel spider are scorpions, toads and bats. Because they also nocturnal, they are active when the camel spider is out hunting for its prey.

A scorpion has the ability to overpower the camel spider and eat it. There are desert toads that are of the same size or bigger than a camel spider so they also have the ability to capture a camel spider for them to eat. On the other and. the bat can find a camel spider by echolocation and swoop down to catch it for a meal.

Chapter One: Camel Spider Facts and Descriptions

Chapter Two: Choosing and Acquiring a Camel Spider

Once you have decided and chosen a camel spider as your pet, it is now time to search for places where you can acquire this creature.

Places to Find Camel Spider

Chapter Two: Choosing and Acquiring a Camel Spider

Shows and Expos

There are a lot of expos and reptile shows all over the country. As you will see, there is an increase in the number of captive-produced camel spider at these shows. The spider offered and presented at these shows are well-fed, healthy and make an excellent and perfect creature to begin as a pet. Moreover, you can get the rare opportunity to select the camel spier you want to purchase and usually, you can also get the chance to speak with an experienced and knowledgeable breeder or keeper. When purchasing online or having the camel spider shipped to you, there may be a chance of receiving camel spiders that are hand-picked by someone who may not have your best interest at heart. By acquiring your camel spider at the shows and expos, you will be able to get really nice camel spider, you can save from the fees of shipping your desired pet and there is less stress placed on the animal from shipping.

Some of the places where you cand find huge numbers of exciting invertebrates in the Unites States are the National

Chapter Two: Choosing and Acquiring a Camel Spider

Reptile Breeders Expo, the Philadelphia for Dallas in Anaheim, Chicago, and Philadelphia.

Camel Spider Dealers

Some keepers are lucky enough to have a local spider specialist near their places. Usually, these keepers are open for visitors in their facilities. With this, you get the opportunity to see the setups of the breeder and see his or her animals. You can also get and learn some tips and tricks in raising this kind of pet, glean some experience and sometimes gain a new colleague or friend with whom to share issues and ideas. You can find and search for these keepers through a a local university entomology department, local invertebrate or herp society, on the Internet and ads in a reptile magazine.

The Internet

The Internet has quickly become a good source of live animals. There are various websites with classified ad sections where you can buy your desired pet, plants as well

Chapter Two: Choosing and Acquiring a Camel Spider

as supplies, food, cages and food for it. However, there are occasional problems that arise from buying from dishonest and faceless sellers or dealers. When buying online, one didn't get to see the facilities and the animals and most of these Internet sellers or dealers are just buying and reselling animals. On the other hand, these Internet dealers can be a good source of camel spiders. Just try to be careful and inquisitive. When contacting dealers, try to ask plenty of questions. Because these people want to keep you as a future customer by selling you a live animal, they should be willing to answer these questions and spend a little extra time with you. Moreover, ensure that these dealers are giving you a fair price by doing your homework by looking and searching for ads and other sources such as dealer price lists. Most online dealers will be willing to send you photos of your desired animal. Ask about their packing and shipping techniques. Ensure that they sound logical, legal and safe for your desired pet. If the seller is not willing to answer your queries and is rude, just look for other dealers. Usually, these deals turn out being the ones you regret.

Chapter Two: Choosing and Acquiring a Camel Spider

Shipping and Transporting Camel Spiders

There are certain concerns and issues about shipping camel spiders, even with overnight delivery services. There are disposable heat and cold packs, styrofoam-lined boxes and most of these can travel across the country in a day without a problem. As suggested, you may ty to ship and receive your camel spider from April to October. Be cautious during cold nights in winter and even more careful during hot days in summer.

Pet & Specialty Stores

As many people show interest in acquiring spider as pets, you can also find camel spiders in different pet stores. Not only they are selling and offering spiders, scorpion, tarantulas and other invertebrates for pets, but they are also exhibit and present their well-fed and healthy animals in appropriate and inspiring setups. Most of them are giving the correct advice and stocking the best supplies and equipment for their customers. They are using better food and prey items for animals. Many of these shops are installing better

Chapter Two: Choosing and Acquiring a Camel Spider

enclosures such as vertically oriented terrariums, cages with screened sides, screen cages, etc. They also often offer help in constructing perfect and inspired setups for their customers.

Pet shops are the first stop for most people searching for an unusual pet. Even though, many continue to get a bad rap, pet shops have the ability to inspire a first-time keeper with the creative ideas and offer correct procedures in setting up enclosure and proper care for camel spiders.

Choosing A Specific Camel Spider

When you finally discover a camel spider you are interested in buying, make sure to check put the enclosure. Check the water if there is a water dish in the enclosure. It should be clean and free of dead insects. The enclosure should also be free of feces. With these, you are given the idea of how often they are cleaned and how much attention they are receiving. Most stores will allow their personnel to toss in a cricket so you can see if the camel spider has a good feeding response.

Chapter Two: Choosing and Acquiring a Camel Spider

Make sure to check the camel spider you are interested in. Make sure it has all legs (though most invertebrates will grow back damaged or missing legs as they molt). Additionally, make sure it is free of bumps, injuries, etc. Lumps, asymmetrical abdomen and bumps are common signs of parasitic infection, injury or disease. Ask the sell about any guarantee he might offer. Is this guarantee offered in writing? Remember, you might get the animal with no possibility of a refund. In fairness, the seller can't see the care you will offer and so can only guarantee the camel spider's current health.

Chapter Two: Choosing and Acquiring a Camel Spider

Chapter Three: Feeding Your Camel Spider

Feeding camel spiders is simple and straightforward. They are going to need a diet consisting of a variety of live prey: Crickets, roaches, grasshoppers, mealworms, waxworms, flies, moths, and occasionally pink or fuzzy mice may be required.

Small camel spiders will need to be fed small insects and as they grow, they will require larger prey items. We feel strongly that all captive invertebrates should be offered a wide variety of prey rather than just feeding those that are

Chapter Three: Feeding Your Camel Spider

easiest to find at the local pet store or bait shop. Most keepers, particularly those with huge collections, also raise and different kinds of prey in connection with their invertebrate creatures to make sure that they will have continuous supply of prey items that are healthy and well-fed to give the best nutrients for their captive pets. Some feeders such as crickets, fruit flies, and wax moths are especially time-consuming to produce.

Feeding your camel spiders prey items that have been gut-loaded, or fed a very nutritious diet, in the hours or days before feeding them to your pets is the ideal situation. Gut-loading of crickets, roaches, and mealworms with healthy food is an important part of feeding your camel spiders. By feeding (gut-loading) your prey items a healthy diet, these nutrients are transferred to your pet inverts.

Feeding Your Camel Spiders

Be sure that you don't feed your spider ants, which can pinch them and cause injury by injecting formic acid. Flies and crickets that are small in size tend to be their favorite

Chapter Three: Feeding Your Camel Spider

meals, while flies and moths work equally as well since they don't bite and won't be able to harm your spider.

Some owners claim to own camel spiders who enjoy eating silverfish and even webworms. When using crickets, it is important that you don't feed one that is too large, because they do have the ability to bite your spider back. In general, try not to place crickets that are more than 1.5x the length of your spider into the enclosure with them.

Learn about Your Spider's Meal Preferences

Overtime, you will come to discover what your spider likes to eat and what it doesn't like to eat. You will also find it interesting to know that certain spiders will consume crickets starting from the head while others consume them starting from the feed. Some camel spiders may have a preference for flies while others won't even touch them. It is up to you as an owner to discover what your camel spiders enjoys eating the most.

Chapter Three: Feeding Your Camel Spider

Where to Acquire Meals

If you live in a warmer climate, you can always catch your spider's meal outdoors using a butterfly net. However, when it gets colder, you can purchase small crickets and insects form pet stores, which are usually quite affordable. When feeding your spider, simply drop the insect into its cage and wait for the spider to pounce on it. When the spider is finished eating, be sure to remove the shells of the insect so that it doesn't cause the cage to smell.

Gut-loading Crickets and Roaches

Crickets and roaches should be filled with a healthy meal in the hours before you feed them to your invertebrates. We recommend adding a small pile of 5-6 of the items below to the cricket or roach enclosure once a week:

- Romaine lettuce

- Greenleaf and redleaf lettuce

- Mustard greens

Chapter Three: Feeding Your Camel Spider

- Collard greens
- Dandelions
- Green beans
- Yellow squash
- Zucchini
- Carrots (shredded)
- Sweet potato (shredded)
- Apple slices
- Orange slices
- Pears
- Cantaloupe
- Mango
- Papaya
- Oats
- Wheat germ

Chapter Three: Feeding Your Camel Spider

- Corn flour

- Rice cereal baby food

- Powdered milk

- Sunflower seeds (unsalted)

- Bee pollen

- Tropical fish flakes

- Spirulina flakes

Water

Depending on its life in nature, a camel spider will require anything from a damp, humid enclosure with frequent mistings to an arid habitat with low ambient humidity and only its prey item as a source of water. Daily or twice daily spraying may be required for more tropical enclosures. While less frequent spraying or a drip system may be enough for forest enclosures.

Chapter Four: Molting

As your camel spider grows, it will need to molt its old exoskeleton to grow. Spiderlings typically molt once a month and larger spiders will molt once or twice a year. Many species of camel spiders will darken in color in the weeks prior to molting. They will also usually stop feeding and become somewhat lethargic. At this time, a keeper needs to make sure that the area underneath the spider's shelter is

Chapter Four: Molting

humid. This humidity will help ensure that a spider molts successfully. Many captive spiders become injured or die during molting due to inadequate conditions in their enclosures.

Molting is a very delicate process. In the days before molting, a layer of fluid and air will form between the spider's old skin and the new skin developing underneath. When the molt is imminent, a spider will usually web the entrance to its burrow or shelter closed. This keeps unwanted insects out and helps seal some of the humidity inside. The spider will lay down a carpet of white silk web and will typically position itself in the center of this web. The spider will flip over on its back and the process of molting will begin.

The spider will begin gently pumping its legs, pumping blood out into its body. The outer old skin will begin to split, first along the carapace and then along the midline of the abdomen. The spider will begin slowly pulling itself out of the split in the carapace. Once it has removed its cephalothorax and abdomen, it will then gently pull each leg out of the old skin. This is a delicate process and if humidity

Chapter Four: Molting

is too low, a leg may get stuck inside the old skin and the spider may lose that leg. In some cases, a spider will lose a leg or two. At other times, the spider may break off a leg and bleed to death or become stuck in the dry skin and die.

After molting, the spider will be soft and extremely vulnerable to any poking or prodding. Crickets will attack and kill spiders during this time. It will take a while for the spider's new skin and even fangs to harden up. Spiderlings may harden up and begin moving and even eating within a day, while adults may take up to a week to get back to normal.

Molting allows a spider to replace lost legs, to replace the urticating hairs that the spider has kicked off its abdomen, and the females become virgins again.

Chapter Four: Molting

Chapter Five: Housing for Your Camel Spider

In order to have a pet camel spider, it is imperative that you have a place to keep her. The best forms of housing are mason jars, sun tea jars, or an aquarium.

Setting Up Your Terrarium

Chapter Five: Housing for Your Camel Spider

Before you catch your spider, you'll need to set up their home. Follow these steps closely and carefully and you will ensure a safe setup for both you and your pet.

Escape Proofing

Find a container to use as the terrarium that will prove to be virtually impossible to escape from. Keep in mind, though, that it has to be easy enough to open that you can feed your black widow. The best containers are listed below in detail:

Sun Tea Jars

Sun tea jars are safe for use with camel spiders because they are made out of glass or plastic. The lid has a tiny hole with a hatch over it that is suitable for a feeding port. Because there is a spout on the side of the jar, ensure that it is plugged up so the spider cannot crawl out.

Chapter Five: Housing for Your Camel Spider

Critter Keepers

Critter keepers can be easily found at garage sales/thrift stores and can be bought at any pet store. These are intended to hold animals firmly.

Mason Jars

Because camel spiders do not require much room, mason jars are the perfect size for your spider. The lids, however, will require holes in the top.

Just remember: Camel spiders are very stationary, and they are not strong enough to lift anything sitting loosely on your terrarium.

Substrate

The bottom of the container will need dirt or sand to serve as the substrate. Sand contrasts your black widow in color, while dirt holds moisture (however this can lead to

Chapter Five: Housing for Your Camel Spider

mold if humidity is too high). You will be learning more about substrate in a few sections.

Hiding Spots

Camel spiders need privacy, as they are reclusive animals. You can use small flower pots, which can be found at any store with gardening supplies. You can also try driftwood, bark, or rocks if you want to go for a more natural look. and Scenery and reptile caves are another approach, and they can be found and bought at pet stores.

Decorations

This step is entirely optional. Figure out what type of decorations you would like for your spider's terrarium. Just make sure that they are not treated with dangerous chemicals that could possibly kill your camel spider.

Chapter Five: Housing for Your Camel Spider

Heating

Heating is a generally unnecessary thing in terms of black widow care. If you live in an extremely cold region, though, heating could become a must, depending on how cold your house gets.

Temperatures

Black widows are most active during the summer months, so the ideal temperature for them is about 76° F (which is considered 'room temperature'). Most commercial heaters for reptiles are heated between 80° F and 90° F. Always ask the salesperson at your local pet store about the temperatures.

Thermometers

When heating your terrarium, it is vital that you have either an external or internal thermometer in order to monitor the temperature.

Chapter Five: Housing for Your Camel Spider

Heat Pads

Brands such as Zoo Med make heating pads that sit beneath the tank. Make sure that the heating pad isn't near or on anything that could potentially burn or melt.

Warnings

A tank that is too hot or too cold can kill your spider. Always keep an eye on things. We personally do not advise the use of heat pads.

Humidity

Humidity is not vital for a camel spider, but moisture for drinking is. If you have a mesh lid aquarium and have plants, then you will need humidity.

For Terrariums with Mesh Lids

On about a weekly basis, spray the ground with water so it looks moist. If the substrate looks predominantly dry, continue spraying until it looks damp. Make sure that there is

Chapter Five: Housing for Your Camel Spider

no pond of accumulated water to prevent your camel spider from being drown.

Other Containers

If you have a different kind of container, minimize the use of humidity and use a wet cotton ball to serve as an area to drink. Water bowls are death traps for camel spiders, as they can very easily drown (they cannot swim).

Warnings

Never spray your spider. The force from the concentrated spray could harm her and subject her to big amounts of water. Also, make sure that your lid is properly ventilated; otherwise, there is a higher possibility of growing mold. No matter what type of terrarium you use, always check for mold.

Chapter Five: Housing for Your Camel Spider

Lighting

Lighting is not essential for camel spiders being that they are nocturnal creatures. There is no need to use lamps or lighting of any sort for your pet camel spider. In fact, the use of lamps can result in burning your spider/causing it to overheat.

Warnings

Do not place your spider's tank close to windows, because filtered sunlight delivers excessive heat for your camel spiders.

Sticks, Rocks, And Branches

Like most spiders, camel spiders build webs. Because of this, you need to provide a sufficient number of sticks, branches, or rocks for them to build off of, giving them points to connect their web lines to.

Chapter Five: Housing for Your Camel Spider

Sticks

There should be at least one large stick that is lengthy enough that it can rest on one side of the tank with the other end anchored into the ground, creating a diagonal position. Camel spiders love to climb these and create a web in the space below the stick.

Branches

You can get the branches of a bush or tree if you have a larger terrarium, as these have numerous points that your spider can build off of. Manzanita plants offer a extensive array of building points off a singular main branch that can provide your spider with spaces to climb.

Rocks

Rocks can turn out to be smaller points to connect webs to as well as surfaces for your camel spiders to climb on.

Chapter Five: Housing for Your Camel Spider

Substrate And Groundcover

Be it sand, reptile bark, or dirt, camel spiders need to have groundcover. Without it, it would feel like you are living in your house without carpet or floorboards.

Choosing Your Groundcover

Choose on what you will use as a groundcover. It can be sand, reptile bark or dirt. Sand can be obtained from beaches (as long as it is legal) and pet stores. Reptile bark is vended in bricks at pet stores. Dirt can be purchased at all stores that has gardening supplies or can be obtained outside from areas free of pesticides.

Dispersing the Groundcover

Place about 1" to 3" of your chosen groundcover across the base of your terrarium. Ensure that it is distributed or dispersed evenly.

Chapter Five: Housing for Your Camel Spider

Plants

You can plant some plants in the soil if you have a mesh or screen top lid for your terrarium. However, they will require lighting, which is not particularly advised in the care of camel spiders.

Live Plants

Live plants make excellent additions to the enclosures of arboreal species. They not only make attractive enhancements to the enclosure; they provide some moisture and humidity and provide natural resting places for your spiders. Hardy, shade-loving species work best. These include **Sanseveria** species, hardy bromeliads and "air plants", **Pothos** ivy, and English ivy, among others. Large camel spiders will typically travel around their enclosures and trample any plants in with them. Baboon spiders will tend to use plants as a basis for their webbing, but may also dig up the plants while excavating and modifying their environment. Unfortunately, many spiders will cover the plants so thickly with webbing that the plants die.

Chapter Five: Housing for Your Camel Spider

Artificial Plants

Plastic or silk artificial plants make a nice alternative to live plants in the spider enclosure. They add some color and places for shelter, breeding, and egg sac production. Also, webbing and trampling do not adversely affect their health.

Warnings

Do not use gravel or cat litter as ground cover because it can trap dirt or moisture which in turn can harm your camel spider if ingested. Do not also use cedar wood shavings, as this can be toxic to your camel spider.

Camel spider are solitary creatures by nature, and don't need "friends" to live with them in their terrarium.

Chapter Five: Housing for Your Camel Spider

Housing Multiple Spiders

Though convenient, it can actually prove dangerous to house more than one spider together, as a risk of cannibalism comes with doing so.

Territory

If you plan on keeping multiple camel spiders in the same terrarium, you will need an aquarium that provides 5 gallons of space for each spider. This enables them to keep their distance from one another and establish their own territories. They should not turn on one another given that there is sufficient food to go around.

Housing Different Genders

Do not house females and males together unless you plan on breeding your camel spiders. Likewise, it is possible that the male will get eaten by his mate.

Housing Separately Opposed to Together

Chapter Five: Housing for Your Camel Spider

It is highly advised that you do the right thing and house camel spiders singly in smaller containers in order to prevent unnecessary deaths among your spider community.

Chapter Six: Vet Care for Your Camel Spider

Health & First Aid

Bad Molts

Occasionally, camel spiders can experience problems with shedding their old skin. This could be due to malnourishment, too high a temperature setting or too low a humidity percentage.

Chapter Six: Vet Care for Your Camel Spider

Physical injury is generally related to leg damage or loss of all or part of the limb and normally it is the joints that are problematic.

These joints can bleed profusely and if led untreated, this uncontrollable loss can prove fatal for the spider. Camel spider blood, a liquid ranging from a clear/cloudy to pale blue color, is not always successful in fully clotting to sufficiently stem the flow.

However, help is at hand and some keepers have successfully stemmed the outflow by using a proprietary purchased **Superglue.**

Surprisingly, a complete loss of leg (**Autotomy**) does not bleed as profusely as if your spider has lost only a part of its leg. With a part loss, you can force the spider to throw off the remainder, by using a pair of tweezers/forceps. Grasp the femur leg segment closest to the body of the spider and pull at it with an upward motion. Then seal the wound with superglue.

The leg should gradually regenerate over the next couple of molts, unless of course if the spider is an older mature male.

Chapter Six: Vet Care for Your Camel Spider

Mites

Some camel spiders can be seen with small mites on their bodies and although a few are quite normal due to the warm humid conditions of an enclosure, it is only when the number of mites become excessive that they then become a problem.

Vigilance is also required when the female has bred and has produced her egg sac, as her bundle can fall victim to mites.

An enclosure that is too humid will encourage the proliferation of mites.

Treatment:

1. Regulate humidity and temperature.
2. If the infestation is excessive, remove spider and sterilize the enclosure.
3. Mites can carefully and gently be removed from the spider with a cotton bud coated in petroleum jelly.

Chapter Six: Vet Care for Your Camel Spider

Mold and Fungal Infections

Mold can become a problem when the relative humidity is too high and/or the substrate is too damp and ventilation is poor.

If detected early enough and treated the spider can make a full recovery but if the infection spreads to the internal organs, this normally proves fatal.

The visible symptoms usually appear on the tips of the legs, the underside of the abdomen and on the carapace and these appear as yellow and white plumes.

These infections are more common with burrowing spiders that spend the majority of their time hidden in their burrows where the substrate is too damp and ventilation is poor.

Treatment:

1. Remove the spider to a clean dry, well-ventilated enclosure that contains a water dish.

Chapter Six: Vet Care for Your Camel Spider

2. Apply to the infected areas a water-based solution containing 10% Iodine. Betadine is one such solution and be purchased at most pharmacies. It may take several applications before any improvement is noticed.

Parasites

Wild caught specimens are more prone to infestation of internal parasites.

Particularly nasty types of parasites causing undue stress and death for spiders are the Nematode worm (certain species-**Steinernema**- can cause bacterial infestation in camel spiders and can prove lethal to the spider) and Wasp Larvae.

Captive bred in camel spiders are generally free from such internal parasites.

Treatment:

None is yet effective.

Chapter Six: Vet Care for Your Camel Spider

Wounds

As previously stated, a camel spider's blood contains no coagulants meaning that a wound will continue to bleed and could prove fatal.

Treatment:

Super Glue (**Cyanoacrylate**) an instant adhesive, which can be purchased at your local hardware shop, has proved very effective in sealing small wounds and stemming the flow of blood.

Vets use an aseptically produced super glue, which is essentially the same cyanoacrylate glue purchased at the local hardware shop, and this can be used in human and animal surgery.

For larger wounds, a specialist vet would need to be consulted.

Chapter Seven: Breeding Your Camel Spider

Sexing

The males and females of most camel spider species look remarkably alike throughout the majority of their life spans; so identifying the sexes can be extremely difficult, especially for the novice keeper.

Chapter Seven: Breeding Your Camel Spider

Mature females and immature males are virtually identical in exterior appearance although females are generally slightly larger than the immature males. It is not until the male reaches maturity and his ultimate molt, that he looks distinctly different to the female.

It is during the final molting process that the male spider obtains its sexual organs, which are shiny bulb-like structures (**Emboli**) situated underneath the tips of the pedipalps. In many species the male will have mating hooks (**tibial spurs**) on the underside of the long segment of the first pair of walking legs, these two structures (**tibial** apophysis) are used to grab the female's fangs during mating.

Male spiders have additional spinnerets forward of the epigastric furrow and these are connected to **Epiandrous** glands, which produce silk. These fusillades are reliable indicators of gender.

A sure way to sex a mature female is to see if she is carrying an egg sac.

Adult females are generally larger and more heavily built than males. The chelicerae (jaws) will also be bigger and

Chapter Seven: Breeding Your Camel Spider

broader. These differences however, can be quite subtle and may need an experienced keeper or breeder to identify.

The use of a microscope on a recently shed skin can determine the sex.

Examining the **Exuvia** (moult) requires experience, by firstly softening the skin and then carefully unfolding it to expose and make visible the book lungs and the genital opening, which are then stretched flat. The spermathecae are surrounded by the uterus externus and lie above the genital organ opening and between the anterior book lungs.

Structures known as **Spermathecae** (sperm storage receptacles) will only be found in female specimens. Be aware however, that some male species have accessory organs, which are a pair of small glands that can be mistaken for spermathecae, but these are always seen as having significantly narrower bases.

Breeding

Experience and knowledge are required to successfully breed camel spiders.

Chapter Seven: Breeding Your Camel Spider

The sex of the two spiders must be determined and a true pair of your preferred species is required before attempting to mate the two spiders.

Time is of the essence where a female camel spider is concerned and to heighten the chances of a successful mating, the introduction of a suitably sperm charged male should be timed as soon as possible after the female has recently molted.

The male spider once motivated to mate, will spin a web on a flat surface or at an angle of about 45 degrees in an enclosure, climb underneath, turn onto his back, rub it's abdomen on the web and deposit a quantity of semen. It will then suck/absorb the sperm into the emboli, the bulb-like features at the tip of its pedipalps, and keep it viable until a receptive female can be found.

The sperm charged male should always be introduced into the female's cage and not visa versa.

They will then begin to display to each other. These exchange signals are to establish if they are of the same species. Surprisingly, the display can be audible and is due to the spiders vibrating their pedipalps and legs against the

Chapter Seven: Breeding Your Camel Spider

substrate. This display may go on for some time, so patience is required.

The displaying couple will gradually approach each other and if the female is receptive, the male will bodily lift the female upwards, and grasps her fangs using his mating hooks and will then insert one of the bulb-like structures (emboli) at the end of his pedipalps into an opening in the lower abdomen (through her epigastric furrow) called the **Opisthosoma.** Once the semen has been transferred, the male will quickly retreat and put some distance between him and the female. The whole procedure can be repeated as sometimes only one of the emboli is used. Although the female can become aggressive after mating, contrary to popular belief, it is quite rare for the male to become a meal. It may be that, as the male gets older, less virile and less potent that there is the possibility that he could end up being dinner for the female.

Providing the male constructs a new sperm web and successfully replenishes his emboli with fresh semen each time, he can then be introduced and mated with several suitable females.

Chapter Seven: Breeding Your Camel Spider

During the whole mating procedure, it is advisable to have to hand a piece of card or plastic that can be used to separate the two spiders if necessary.

Some other tips for successful breeding of many species of camel spiders include:

The Enclosure

For successful breeding, females of many terrestrial species seem to require a deep burrow. This can be achieved by simply starting a burrow for the spider in deep substrate and allowing it to dig further and reinforce the burrow with its own webbing. Another method is to create an artificial burrow via a plastic tube such as those used for gerbils or hamsters. Burrows can also be produced from a piece of clay pipe or one can be carved in a large piece of furniture foam which can be inserted into the enclosure. There are a wide variety of "burrows" in use by keepers worldwide and there are no limits to what can be created. The burrow not only provides the spider with a more natural home and less stressful microhabitat, it also provides the female spiders a

Chapter Seven: Breeding Your Camel Spider

safe, stress-free place to produce and to nurture an egg sac. Those breeders who have been most successful in breeding terrestrial species, commonly provide their adult female spiders burrows in which to live.

Conditioning

A keeper who keeps his or her spiders healthy (not obese) is more likely to produce viable eggsacs with higher hatching rates. As with most captive animals, overfeeding and obesity are common. It appears that the same can be said for captive spiders too. Often keepers enjoy seeing their captives eat and this leads to overfeeding. We feel that by feeding an adult spider once a week and feeding a variety of healthy prey items, a spider can be kept healthier and is more likely to live longer and produce more and healthier spiderlings when bred.

"Seasonal" Changes

Chapter Seven: Breeding Your Camel Spider

As our knowledge of the keeping and breeding of camel spiders in captivity improves, it appears that manipulation of environmental temperature can be important to stimulate breeding in spiders from temperate areas. Some of the more tropical tree spiders may also benefit greatly from a mild cooling period and by a change in seasons from dry to wet. We feel that a keeper should investigate the natural environment for each species he or she keeps. A weather report for each month of the year can be found on-line. This weather information can give the keeper an idea of the ideal situation for a captive specimen and what triggers might stimulate members of this species to reproduce in captivity.

Eggs and Spiderlings

It is dependent upon the species of camel spider as to the time that the female will lay her eggs. It could be a few weeks or even months. Females can lay 50 -200 plus eggs, which she will deposit into an egg sac, a silken web bundle that she has spun, and she will then fertilize them using the males sperm which she has stored ready for her egg laying. The female will be very protective of her silken bundle. As the

Chapter Seven: Breeding Your Camel Spider

eggs develop, the female will periodically rotate her precious egg sac and this action called **Brooding** helps to keep the eggs from deforming.

If the egg bundle is infertile, the female will instinctively know this and will abandon it. However, the female will sometimes put the sac down to feed. Do not disturb it unless it has been left for a disproportionate length of time.

It is possible to check if her eggs are indeed infertile. By careful opening of the egg sac, you will notice that infertile eggs will be the same yellow/white color as when they were laid. If, however, they have dark features and shadows, they could possibly still be fertile. If this is the case then the next course of action is to consider artificial incubation.

The egg bundle should be resealed and placed in a separate container, which must be kept at a constant humidity of 75% and a temperature of 79 degrees F (26C).

As in nature, the bundle must be rotated frequently to stop the eggs from becoming deformed.

Chapter Seven: Breeding Your Camel Spider

Constant vigilance is certainly called for, as the job of breaking open the bundle and releasing the spiderlings is a task that you will have to undertake.

Depending upon the species, spiderlings can take between 2 – 12 weeks to hatch, hence the constant vigilance required.

These baby spiders will not eat straight from hatching, as they can survive on their egg yolk, which will be absorbed.

They will have experienced their first molt inside the egg nest and it is only after the second molt (first outside the egg sac) that they will gradually disperse and explore the enclosure looking for food. Now is the time to catch and separate them and individually re-house them lest they begin to eat each other.

Egg Sacs

After a successful pairing, the female camel spider now has sperm stored in her spermathecae, or sperm storing organs. These spermathecae are pockets located just under the female's genital opening. After a varying period of time,

Chapter Seven: Breeding Your Camel Spider

the female will be ready to lay her eggs. The process of egg-laying is similar for most species. The female will first lay out a small carpet of thick, white web. Upon this web carpet she will lay from 50 to as many as 250 small eggs. The eggs are fertilized by the male's sperm as they pass the spermathecae. Once she has completed the egg-laying, she will pull the corners of the web carpet into a small packet containing the eggs.

This egg sac prevents predators from getting to the eggs and also helps seal in humidity. Depending on the species, the egg sac is either suspended within the burrow or a tube web or is transformed into a loose ball-shaped package that is carried around by the female. In these cases, the egg sac is grasped firmly in her chelicerae, or fangs, and is manipulated by the first pair of legs.

Those species that carry their egg sac around will often move the egg sac in and out of the burrow or tube web to expose the eggs to the proper warmth and humidity within the enclosure.

Chapter Seven: Breeding Your Camel Spider

Most species will only lay one egg sac after a successful pairing. Occasionally, a female will lay two clutches of fertile eggs. When a female camel spider molts, she sheds the lining of the spermathecae, losing the sperm stored there, and thus loses the ability to produce fertile eggs.

To Take or Not to Take the Egg Sac

Most successful spider breeders will allow a female to carry her egg sac for a month to six weeks and then will take the egg sac away from her.

Occasionally, when an enclosure is in a room with lots of traffic or if the enclosure is bumped, a female may become stressed and eat the egg sac and eggs within. This is a frustrating experience and after several losses, a breeder often decides to take the egg sac and incubate it away from the female.

The key to incubating an egg sac is having a system in place that has worked successfully. We have used a simple setup using two large plastic tubs. This incubation setup has

Chapter Seven: Breeding Your Camel Spider

worked for a wide range of species and is simple and inexpensive. First, a keeper should fill a 6" to 8" diameter deli tub with 1-2" of damp peat moss (mix water and peat moss together and squeeze the excess water out). Over this tub is placed another tub from which the bottom has been removed with a sharp knife. On this top tub is placed a sheet of cheese cloth which is secured tightly with a rubber band or wire. The egg sac sits gently on the piece of cheese cloth, suspended above the humid substrate. This allows the egg sac to be kept humid, but keeps it up off the substrate to prevent it from getting too damp and getting moldy.

This setup is placed in a warm room (75° to 80° F) in a larger plastic sweater box with plenty of ventilation holes for the remaining incubation time. In the first weeks, the egg sac is gently rolled by the keeper six to eight times per day to keep the eggs within from clumping together.

The egg sac should not be taken from a female while the eggs are very recently laid. When the eggs are laid, the coats the eggs, providing them with humidity and probably containing substances that dissuade any would be predatory

Chapter Seven: Breeding Your Camel Spider

flies and other small attackers. The female camel spider gently rolls the egg sac and the eggs within while she carries it with her. This rolling prevents the liquid and egg mass from sticking together and clumping. If an egg sac is taken too soon and the egg sac is placed on the cheese cloth, the eggs and liquid will clump together, killing the developing eggs. Once the small nymphs begin to develop, this liquid is absorbed and will no longer cause the small spiders to clump together. An experienced breeder will be able to tell from the changing shape of the egg sac and by the feel of the small nymphs inside. The egg sac will feel looser and the ball of nymphs will be more spread out within the egg sac, telling the keeper that the nymphs are moving around somewhat. It is at this time that the keeper can remove the egg sac to a support structure to carefully watch the further development of the nymphs and to prevent a female, especially of a very rare species, from destroying what has been months or even years of hard work and preparation.

The nymphs of camel spiders look like light-colored peas with small, stubby legs. After a period of time, they will molt and look more like small, mobile spiders. Nymphs of

Chapter Seven: Breeding Your Camel Spider

Some species will remain within the egg sac until they molt their skins for the first time. At this time, they will emerge from the egg sac and spend some time together. Once they are mobile and ready to begin feeding, they will usually disperse into the enclosure and seek out a small space to begin their daily routine of waiting for food.

Spiderlings of many species will begin cannibalizing their siblings. They should soon be removed to small, individual containers.

Caring For Egg Sacs

If you are lucky enough to witness your camel spider spinning a large resting sac, and then inserting a mass of eggs in it, you should understand how to care for the egg sacs. A lot of the times, you will find that their egg sacs are so well hidden that you won't even realize that there are any eggs until the babies start emerging.

You will need to make sure that the outer part of the egg sacs don't become too dry. This can be done by misting them once per week using a small spray bottle. Avoid

Chapter Seven: Breeding Your Camel Spider

spraying in the direction where the entrance of the sac is located. Make sure that there aren't babies emerging, or you could drown them while misting.

How Long Before Babies Become Visible?

It can take anywhere between two and four weeks before the babies in the sac start to become visible. They will start shedding their skin while within the sac before emerging. Allow the baby spiders to exit the sac on their own.

It may take as an entire month before all of the babies have left the sac. As they exit, they will be quite easy to blow into a cup (using the same strength as if you were blowing out a candle). Don't touch them or you will certainly kill them- they are simply too delicate to be handled at this point. The air-blowing method should never hurt them, and will be a safe way to transport them to another container if needed.

Chapter Seven: Breeding Your Camel Spider

Housing

Initially baby spiders can be housed in small cages (slightly higher ones required for arboreal species). Fill to approximately a third of the height with a good moist fine substrate. In the case of arboreal species, it is recommended to insert a few upright twigs. The enclosure must be ventilated and secure to stop the spiderling from escaping.

Plastic Containers

Plastic containers such as vials, deli cups, sandwich tubs, shoe boxes, and pint jars are available to provide a variety of sizes and shapes for spiderling enclosures. They are typically inexpensive and easy to find at any local department store. When used for keeping invertebrates, it is best to alter the lids or sides of these containers to permit the airflow. For spiderlings, these air holes need to be quite small and can be made with a small, sharp nail, a needle, or other tool.

Substrate

Chapter Seven: Breeding Your Camel Spider

Young spiders are easier kept on a "light-weight" substrate. We keep most burrowing species in vials or small containers filled about halfway with peat moss with a pinch of sphagnum moss on top. This moss "plug" will give the spiderling a place to attach some webs and will help hold in moisture. The moss is easy to moisten and dries out more naturally. The peat and sphagnum will also lighten in color when dry, giving the keeper an idea of when water needs to be added to the vial. Heavier substrates such as sand can settle onto the spiderling if the vial is bumped or jostled, killing the spiderling. Many keepers use paper towel as a substrate for spiderlings. It is both easy to clean and is slow to support the growth of mold and fungus which kills many captive spiderlings. It does, however, dry out quickly and a keeper must be diligent to not let the inside of the container become too dry. Dehydration kills many spiderlings.

Now separately rehomed, temperature and humidity levels are critical.

Chapter Seven: Breeding Your Camel Spider

Temperature

A temperature of 79 degrees F (26C) constant is necessary.

Too low a temperature and the spiderlings will not eat and will therefore starve.

Too high a temperature and the spiderlings will suffocate and die.

Humidity

A humidity of 75% is necessary.

Too low a humidity % can cause the spiderlings to suffocate.

Too high a humidity % can cause a problem with too much condensation forming on the sides of the housing making the substrate too wet. Spiderlings can also become trapped in condensate, which can also prove fatal.

Chapter Seven: Breeding Your Camel Spider

Food

Feed the spiderlings as often as it is accepted with suitable food and under this feeding routine, spiderlings will rapidly grow. At this stage of their development, molting (shedding their skin) can be as often as once per month, which is quite common.

Conclusion

Thank you for reading. I hope this camel spider pet guide has provided you with the right tools and knowledge on how to keep and raise your spider pet healthy and appropriately.

Enjoy your camel spiders! It is miraculous that some of them, so incredibly small as spiderlings, grow into the large, aggressive, hairy beasts that we enjoy so much.

Habitats across the planet are under attack. With the destruction of forests comes the loss of spiders. The spiders in captive breeding programs across the planet are potentially the only source for future populations of camel spiders, both for the hobby and for possible reintroduction into "recovered" ecosystems.

Keeping healthy spiders in creative enclosures will not only inspire others who visit your collection, but will also provide the potential for breeding and production of healthy spiderlings to share with other keepers.

Conclusion

I suggest that you make contact with other keepers - trade, sell, buy, and enjoy the unusual hobby of spider keeping and breeding!

Glossary of Terms

Abdomen- The posterior (rear) of the two major divisions of the body of a spider.

Accessory claws- Serrated, thickened hairs near the true claws in some spiders.

Anal tubercle- A small projection, dorsal to the spinners, carrying the anal opening.; the small caudal tubercle bearing the anal opening; the postabdomen.

Annulations- Rings of pigmentation around leg segments.

Antennae- The segmented sensory organs often termed "feelers," borne on the heads of insects, crustacea, et cetera , but missing in all arachnids.

Glossary of Terms

Anterior- Nearer the front or head end.

Appendages- Parts or organs (such as legs, spinnerets, chelicerae) that are attached to the body.

Arachnida- A principal division, or Class, of the air-breathing arthropods, the arachnids, including the scorpions, mites, spiders, harvestmen, etc.

Arachnologist- One who studies the arachnids.

Araneae- The ordinal name of all spiders; same as Araneida.

Araneology- The branch of zoology that treats only of the spiders. Arthropod.The jointed-legged animals, such as centipedes, millipedes, insects, crustaceans, spiders, scorpions, and many other less well-known types; the members of the Phylum Arthropoda.

Glossary of Terms

Attachment disc- The series of tiny lines that serve to anchor the draglines of spiders.

Autophagy- The eating of an appendage shed from the body by autotomy or otherwise.

Autospasy- The loss of appendages by breaking them at a predetermined locus of weakness when pulled by an outside form; frequent in spiders and arachnids.

Autotomy- The act of reflex self-mutilation by dropping appendages; unknown in the arachnids.

Ballooning- Flying through the air on silken lines spun by spiders.; aeronautical dispersal by means of air currents acting on strands of silk.

Book lung- An air-filled cavity, containing stacks of blood-filled leaves, opening on the underside of the abdomen.; the respiratory pouches of the arachnids, filled with closely packed sheets or folds to provide maximum surface for aeration; believed to be modified, insunk gills.

Branchial operculum- A sclerotized, hairless plate overlying the book lung.

Calamistrum- The more -or less extensive row of curved hairs on the hind metatarsi, used to comb the silk from the cribellum.; a comb-like series of hairs on metatarsus IV of cribellate spiders

Carapace- The hard dorsal covering of the cephalothorax in the Arachnida; the exoskeletal covering, or shell, over the dorsal (upper) surface of the cephalothorax.

Cardiac mark- An elongate midline mark on the anterior, dorsal surface of the abdomen which overlies the heart.

Glossary of Terms

Catalepsy- The action of feigning death; induced by disturbance.

Cephalothorax- The united head and thorax of Arachnida and Crustacea.; the anterior (front) of the two major divisions of the body of a spider.

Chelicerae- The pincerlike first pair of appendages of the arachnids; in spiders two-segmented, the distal portion or fang used to inject venom from enclosed glands into the prey.; the jaws, each one comprising a large basal part and a fang

Chitin- A linear homopolysaceharide found as the characteristic molecule in the cuticle of arthropods. The molecules are layered in chains and cross-linked to form the strong, lightweight basis of the cuticle.

Chorion- The outer covering or shell of the spider or insect egg.

Glossary of Terms

Claw tuft- A bunch of hairs at the tip of the leg tarsus in spiders with only two claws.; the pair of tufts of adhesive hairs present below the paired claws at the tip of the tarsi of many spiders.

Clypeus- The area between the anterior row of eyes and the anterior edge of the carapace.

Colulus- The slender or pointed appendage immediately in front of the spinnerets of some spiders; in other greatly reduced or seemingly missing; the homologue of the anterior median spinnerets or cribellum.; a small midline appendage or tubercle arising just in front of the anterior spinners in some spiders.

Conductor- A semi-membranous structure in the male palp which supports and guides the embolus in insemination.

Glossary of Terms

Condyle- A smooth, rounded protuberance sometimes present on the outer side of the chelicera, near its base.

Coxa- The basal segment of the leg by means of which it is articulated to the body; the segment of leg nearest the body; modified in the palp to form the maxilla.

Coxal glands- The excretory organs of arachnids, in spiders located opposite the coxae of the first and third legs, that collect wastes into a saccule and discharge them through tubes opening behind the coxae; homologous with the nephridia of Peripatus, etc.

Cribellum- A sievelike, transverse plate, usually divided by a delicate keel into two equal parts, located in front of the spinnerets of many spiders; the modified anterior median spinnerets.; a spinning organ just in front of the spinners which appears as a transverse plate. Only present in cribellate spiders, which also have a calamistrum.

Glossary of Terms

Cuticle- The hard outer covering of an arthropod.

Cymbium- The broadened, hollowed-out tarsus of the male palp within which the palpal organs are attached.

Deutovum- The resting, spiderlike stage following the shedding of the chorion of the egg; the second egg.

Distal- Pertaining to the outer end, furthest away from the body or point of attachment.

Dorsal- Pertaining to the upper surface.

Dorsum- In general, the upper surface.

Ecdysis- The process of casting the skin; molting.

Glossary of Terms

Embolus- The structure, in the male palp, containing the terminal part of the ejaculatory duct and its opening. It may be very small, or long, whip-like or coiled and is sometimes divided into several structures.

Endite- The plate borne by the coxa of the pedipalps of most spiders, used to crush the prey; the maxilla.

Entelegyne- The group of spiders in which the females have an epigyne.

Epigastric fold- A fold and groove separating the anterior part of the ventral abdomen (with epigyne and book lungs) from the posterior part.

Epigyne- A more or less sclerotized and modified external structure associated with the reproductive openings of adult females of most spider species.

Glossary of Terms

Epigynum- The more or less complicated apparatus for storing the spermatozoa, immediately in front of the opening of the internal reproductive organs of female spiders.

Exoskeleton- The hard, external, supportive covering found in all arthropods.

Exuviae- The parts of cuticle cast off during moulting.

Fang- The claw-like part of each chelicera; the poison duet opens near its tip.

Femur- The thigh; usually the stoutest segment of the spider's leg, articulated to the body through the trochanter and coxa and bearing the patella and remaining leg segments at its distal end.

Folium- Any pattern of pigment on the dorsum of the abdomen which is fairly broad and leaf-shaped.

Glossary of Terms

Fovea- A short median groove on the thoracic part of the carapace which marks the internal attachment of the gastric muscles.

Genitalia- All the genital structures.

Gossamer- A light film of silk threads, or groups of these floating through the air.

Hackled band- The composite threads of the cribellate spiders, spun by cribellum and combed by the calamistrum.

Haematodocha- A balloon of elastic connective tissue between groups of seletites in the male palp which distends with blood during insemination causing the selerites to separate and rotate.

Glossary of Terms

Haplogyne- The group of spiders in which the females have no epigyne.

Head- The part of the carapace carrying the eyes which is separated from the thorax by a shallow groove.

Labium- The lip, under the mouth opening and between the maxillae, attached to the front of the sternum.

Lanceolate- Tapering to a point.

Lateral- Pertaining to the side.

Lyriform organ- A sensory organ near the distal end of limb segments formed of a group of parallel slit organs.

Maxilla- The mouthparts on each side of the labium which are the modified coxae of the palps..

Glossary of Terms

Median- In the midline or middle.

Median apophysis- A selerite arising from the middle division of the male palpal organs.

Metatarsus- (pl. metatarsi; adj. metatarsal) The sixth segment of the leg, counting from the body.

Orb web- A two-dimensional web, roughly circular in design (and, strictly speaking, a misnomer). Silk threads radiate like spokes from a central hub. These are then overlaid with a spiral of silk, running from the periphery almost to the hub.

Palp- Short for pedipalp. The appendage arising just in front of the legs, the coxa of which also forms the maxilla. It has no metatarsal segment and in adult males is greatly modified for the transfer of semen.

Glossary of Terms

Palpal organs- The more or less complex structures fs)und in the terminal part of the adult male palp. They comprise groups of sclerites separated from each other and the cymbium by up to three haematodochac and contain the semen reservoir which opens via ducts through the tip of the embolus.

Paracymbium- A structure in the male palp branching from, or loosely attached to, the cymbium.

Patella- (pl. Patellae, (adj. patellar) The fourth segment of the leg or palp, counting from the body.

Pedicel- The narrow stalk connecting the cephalothorax and the abdomen.

Pheromone- A chemical secreted by an animal in minute amounts which brings about a behavioral response in another, often of the opposite sex.

Glossary of Terms

Phylogenetic- Pertaining to evolutionary relationships between and within groups.

Posterior- Near the rear end.

Process- A projection from the main structure.

Procurved- Curved as an arc having its ends ahead of its center.

Prolateral- Projecting from, or on, the side facing forwards.

Proximal- Pertaining to the inner end; closest to the body or point of attachment.

Punctate- Covered with tiny depressions.

Glossary of Terms

Recurved- Curved as an arc having its ends behind its center.

Reticulated- Like network.

Retrolateral- Projecting from, or on, the side facing backwards.

Rugose- Rough, wrinkled.

Scape- A finger-, tongue-, or lip-like projection from the midline of the female epigyne.

Sclerite- Any separate sclerotized structure connected to other structures by membranes.

Sclerotized- Hardened or horny; not flexible or membranous.

Glossary of Terms

Scopula- (pl. scopulae) A brush of hairs on the underside of the tarsus and metatarsus in some spiders.

Scutum- A hard, often shiny, sclerotized plate on the abdomen of some spiders.

Septum- A partition separating two cavities or parts.

Serrated- Saw-toothed.

Sexual dimorphism- A difference in form, color, size, etc., between sexes of the same species.

Sigillum- (pl. sigilla) An impressed, sclerotized spot, often reddish-brown. Often present on the dorsal surface of the abdomen and marking points of internal muscle attachments.

Slit organ- A stress receptor in the exoskeleton

Glossary of Terms

Sperm induction- The process of transferring the spermatozoa from the genital orifice beneath the base of the abdomen into the receptacle in the male palpus.

Sperm web- A web of few or many threads on which male spiders deposit the semen preparatory to taking it into the palpus.

Spermathecae- The vessels or receptacles in the epigyna of female spiders that store the spermatozoa of the males.; the sacs or cavities in female spiders which receive and store semen.

Spermatozoa- The mature sperm cells.

Spiderling- A tiny, immature spider, usually the form just emerged from the egg sac.; the nymphal or immature spider,

Glossary of Terms

generally resembling the adult, hut smaller; fully mobile and no longer dependent on yolk.

Spine-A thick, stiff hair or bristle.

Spinnerets- The fingerlike abdominal appendages of spiders through which the silk is spun.

Spinners- Paired appendages at the rear end of the abdomen, below the anal tubercle, from the spigots of which silk strands are extruded.

Spiracle-A breathing pore or orifice leading to tracheae or book lungs.; the opening of the tracheae on the underside of the abdomen.

Stadium- The interval between the molts of arthropods; instar; a period in the development of an arthropod.

Glossary of Terms

Sternum- A sclerotized plate between the coxae marking the floor of the cephalothorax.; the heart-shaped or oval exoskeletal shield covering the under surface of the cephalothorax.

Stridulating organ- A file-and-scraper for sound production; may be variously located on chelicerae, palps, legs, abdomen and carapace.

Subadult- Almost adult; the last instar before maturity.

Synonym- Each of two or more scientific names of the same rank used to denote the same taxon. The senior synonym is the name first established.

Tarsus- The foot; the most distal segment of the legs, which bears the claws at its tip.; the most distal (or end) segment of a leg or palp.

Glossary of Terms

Taxon- Any taxonomic unit (eg. family, genus, species).

Taxonomy- The theory and practice of classifying organisms, part of systematics, the study of the kinds and diversity of organisms.

Tergites- Dorsal sclerites on the body; the hard plates on the abdomen of the atypical tarantulas that indicate the segmentation.

Thorax- The second region of the body of insects that bears the legs; in spiders, fused with the head to form the cephalothorax.; that part of the cephalothorax behind the head region andseparated from it by a shallow groove.

Tibia- pl. Tibiae adj. tibial) The fifth segment of the leg or palp counting from the body.

Glossary of Terms

Tracheae- The air tubes in insects; in spiders, tubular respiratory organs of different origin; by many thought to be modified book lungs.; tubes through which air is carried around the body and which open at the spiracles.

Trichobothrium- (pl. trichobothria) A long, fine hair rising almost vertically from a socket on the leg. Trichobothria detect air vibrations and currents.

Trochanter- The second segment of the leg or palp, counting from the body.

Ventral- Pertaining to the underside.

Zygote- The fertilized egg.

Index

A

abdomen 23, 42
acquire 9
appearance 46
aquarium 25
arachnid 7

B

babies 6
breed 47
breeder 11, 47, 58
breeding 50
bumps 15
buying 14

C

cages 14, 61
carapace 23
carnivores 7
cephalothorax 23
chemicals 28
color 3
containers 26
cricket 14

D

dealers 12

Index

decorations 28
desert 4
diet 17

E

egg sacs 7
eggs 6, 52
enclosure 18
enclosures 23
equipment 13
exoskeleton 6

F

feeding 16
females 45
food 8, 64

G

gender 46
groundcover 34

H

habitat 4, 21
hatching 51
hatchlings 6
health 15
heating 29
heating pads 30
housing 25
humidity 21, 28, 30, 63

Index

I

incubation	53
infection	15, 42
injuries	15
injury	40
invertebrates	10

J

jars	25

K

keepers	11

L

leg 40

lifecycle	5
lighting	32

M

male	37
mating	4
meal	19
mites	41
molt	22
molting	22, 46
mother	6
mouth	3

Index

N

nest 54
nocturnal 4
nutrients 17
nymphs 58

P

parasites 43
pedipalps 3, 48
pet stores 13
plants 35
predators 3, 8
prey 3, 7, 16
purchase 10

S

setup 26, 57
shedding 39
shipping 10, 13
size 4
skin 24, 47, 60
species 47
spiderlings 54
spraying 30
substrate 28, 61
sun spider 2
supplies 13, 34

T

temperature 29, 52, 63

Index

temperatures 5
terrariums 14

V

ventilation 57

W

water 14
weight 4
wind scorpion 2

Index

Photo Credits

Page 2, Willem Van Zyl via Canva.com (Canva Pro License)

https://www.canva.com/photos/MADRBJh27iE-orange-solifuge-camel-spider-wind-spider-red-roman-closeup-a-harmless-arachnid/

Page 9, ePhotocorp via Canva.com (Canva Pro License)

https://www.canva.com/photos/MAEGP2sk3g8-solifuge-known-variously-as-camel-spiders-wind-scorpions-or-sun-spiders-panna-madhya-pradesh-india/

Page 16, Michael Wallis via Canva.com (Canva Pro License)

https://www.canva.com/photos/MAEORGh5mj4-a-large-camel-spider-eating-a-larger-grasshopper/

Photo Credits

Page 22, ePhotocorp via Canva.com (Canva Pro License)

https://www.canva.com/photos/MAESf4Aori4-solifuge-or-camel-spider-with-kill-jaisalmer-rajasthan-india/

Page 25, quangpraha via Canva.com (Canva Pro License)

https://www.canva.com/photos/MADF0JhacsQ-camel-spiders-paragaleodes-heliophilous-are-large-arachnids-generally-in-habit-warm-and-arid-habitats/

Page 39, Roman_Gilmanov via Canva.com (Canva Pro License)

https://www.canva.com/photos/MADAT-SZioY-camel-spider/

Page 45, Stephane Bidouze via Canva.com (Canva Pro License)

Photo Credits

https://www.canva.com/photos/MADFmlv_St0-giant-spider-molting-and-breeding/

References

Camel Spider: Facts and Myths – Livescience.com

https://www.livescience.com/40025-camel-spiders-facts.html

Camel Spider- Nationalgeographic.com

https://www.nationalgeographic.com/animals/invertebrates/facts/camel-spider

Camel Spider – Biologydictionary.net

https://biologydictionary.net/camel-spider/

Sunspider- Britannica.com

https://www.britannica.com/animal/sunspider

Camel Spider - Ddcr.org

https://www.ddcr.org/florafauna/Detail.aspx?Class=Arthropods&Referrer=Solifugae&Subclass=Spiders%20and%20Scorpions&Id=12

Camel Spider- A-z-animals.com

https://a-z-animals.com/animals/camel-spider/

Egyptian Giant Solpugid (Camel Spider) - animalofthewould.fandom.com

https://animalofthewould.fandom.com/wiki/Egyptian_Giant_Solpugid_(Camel_Spider)

Tailless Whipscorpions & Sun Spiders - Desertmuseum.org

https://www.desertmuseum.org/books/nhsd_whipscorpions.php

Solpugids - Desertusa.com

https://www.desertusa.com/insects/solpugids.html

Solifugae: Formidable Order Of The Sun Spider & Wind Scorpion – Earthlife.net

https://www.earthlife.net/chelicerata/sunscorp.html

Camel Spider - Animals.net

https://animals.net/camel-spider/

Camel Spider Facts - Softschools.com

https://www.softschools.com/facts/animals/camel_spider_facts/1848/

Spider Feeding – Spidersworlds.com

https://www.spidersworlds.com/spider-feeding/

What Do Spiders Eat? - Terminix.com

https://www.terminix.com/blog/education/what-do-spiders-eat/

What do Spiders Eat - Earthkind.com

https://www.earthkind.com/blog/what-do-spiders-eat-the-diet-of-a-common-house-spider/

Breeding - Giantspiders.com

https://www.giantspiders.com/captive-care/breeding/

.org/

Spider Reproduction 101: Just How Do Spiders Mate? – Earthlife.net

https://www.earthlife.net/chelicerata/s-reproduce.html

Spider Reproduction, Growth And Development - Biodiversityexplorer.info

https://www.biodiversityexplorer.info/arachnids/spiders/reproduction.htm

www.ingramcontent.com/pod-product-compliance
Lightning Source LLC
Chambersburg PA
CBHW070540080426
42453CB00029B/789